This Book Belongs To:

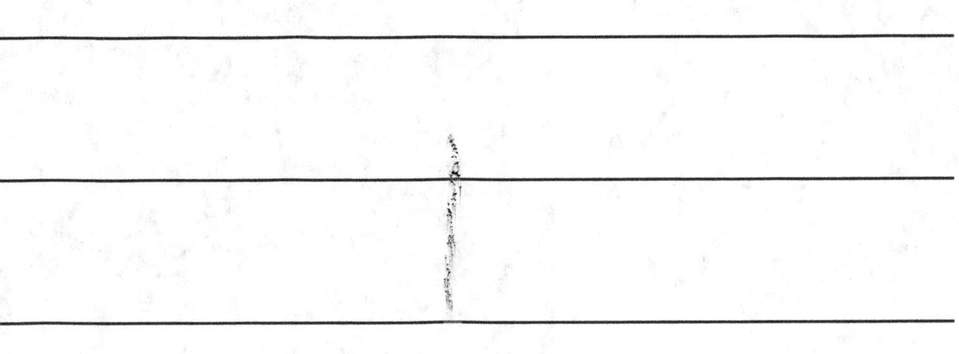

____

____

____

Today's Lesson
Learning
Sight
Words

Enjoy Learning Sight Words

Color The Word	Trace The Word

Find and Circle The Word

This is a new house.

A bike rode down the street.

I will go on a trip.

an   a   a   e   a   u   I   a   are

Read The Word	Write The Word
I see **a** cat and **a** dog.	

Write the Word in a Sentence

Can I have _____ cookie?

Don't Forget to Give Yourself the Rates.

Enjoy Learning Sight Words

Color The Word	Trace The Word
am	am

Find and Circle The Word

I am a big brother.	we　　am
You are tall, but I am not.	am　　made
Am I ready for bed?	me　　me
	mom am　　am

Read The Word	Write The Word
a　l　k　m	

Write the Word in a Sentence

I _____ in love with her.

Don't Forget to Give Yourself the Rates. 

Enjoy Learning Sight Words

Color The Word	Trace The Word
and	and

Find and Circle The Word

And how old are you?

She runs and he does too.

Cats and dogs are pets.

ant
and
can
ball
man
land
and
art
and

Read The Word	Write The Word
p n e a z d	

Write the Word in a Sentence

You _______ I are kids.

Don't Forget to Give Yourself the Rates. 

Enjoy Learning Sight Words

Color The Word	Trace The Word
are	are

Find and Circle The Word

We are family.

Are we there yet?

They are my dogs.

have   are
are   far
are
bare   can
arm   are

Read The Word	Write The Word
d r i a s e	

Write the Word in a Sentence

We _______ friends.

Don't Forget to Give Yourself the Rates.

Enjoy Learning Sight Words

Color The Word	Trace The Word
at	at

Find and Circle The Word

At the park I see a slide.

She was at school today.

We stay at home.

at   at

hat   it

tan   to

at   of   at

Read The Word	Write The Word
a p i t	

Write the Word in a Sentence

Are you _______ the zoo?

Don't Forget to Give Yourself the Rates. 

Enjoy Learning Sight Words

Color The Word	Trace The Word
be	be

Find and Circle The Word

Will you be my friend?

She can be kind.

Can I be in the middle?

be   can   be   she   bed   bee   the   be   be

Read The Word	Write The Word
s e b t	

Write the Word in a Sentence

I will _______ there.

Don't Forget to Give Yourself the Rates.

Enjoy Learning Sight Words

Color The Word	Trace The Word
big	big

Find and Circle The Word

Do you have a big sister?

I live in a big house.

Fish can be big or small.

big bite bay big day big dig big bat big

Read The Word	Write The Word
k i g b q h	

Write the Word in a Sentence

That is a very _______ tree.

Enjoy Learning Sight Words

Color The Word	Trace The Word
but	but

Find and Circle The Word

She likes dogs, but not cats. He goes anywhere but home. I can ski, but she cannot.	but but hat tub dot bat but put but

Read The Word	Write The Word
s u t b e r	

Write the Word in a Sentence

I like red, _______ not blue.

Don't Forget to Give Yourself the Rates. 

Enjoy Learning Sight Words

Color The Word	Trace The Word
can	can

Find and Circle The Word

I can read.

Can you tell me a story?

Cats can be funny.

van can can to can cake man can cat

Read The Word	Write The Word
c z n p a y	

Write the Word in a Sentence

I ______ do this!

Don't Forget to Give Yourself the Rates. 

Enjoy Learning Sight Words

Color The Word

come

Trace The Word

come

Find and Circle The Word

Come on, let's go.

I will come to the zoo with you.

We come from this town.

won
come
come
on
come
mom
come
came
come

Read The Word

g o m r

c s w e

Write The Word

Write the Word in a Sentence

Will you __________ to my party?

Don't Forget to Give Yourself the Rates.

Enjoy Learning Sight Words

Color The Word

day

Trace The Word

day

Find and Circle The Word

I love reading day and night.
During the day, we drink milk.
What day is your birthday?

dot   date
bay   daze
day   day
day   bat   day

Read The Word

d   u   y

t   a   r

Write The Word

Write the Word in a Sentence

What _______ is today?

Enjoy Learning Sight Words

Color The Word	Trace The Word
do	do

Find and Circle The Word

We do the dishes.

What can I do for you?

Do your dogs bark?

doll   do   pot   boat   do   to   do   do   deer

Read The Word	Write The Word
r o d w	

Write the Word in a Sentence

We _____ our best.

Don't Forget to Give Yourself the Rates. 

Enjoy Learning Sight Words

Color The Word	Trace The Word
down	down

Find and Circle The Word

What goes up, comes down.

He is down and out.

We walk down the path.

won   down
down
down   paw
do   down   done   down

Read The Word	Write The Word
d o t r / m s w n	

Write the Word in a Sentence

Let's ski _________ the slope.

Enjoy Learning Sight Words

Color The Word	Trace The Word

for

Find and Circle The Word

What are you waiting for?

I use a pencil for writing.

This cup is for water.

for   war   fat   for   from   far   roll   for   for

Read The Word	Write The Word

n   o   r

f   w   d

Write the Word in a Sentence

This gift is _____ my dad.

Don't Forget to Give Yourself the Rates.

Enjoy Learning Sight Words

Color The Word	Trace The Word
go	go

Find and Circle The Word

| We will go to bed.
Let's go to John.
Can I go now? | off go
go goat
go
jug go got go |

Read The Word	Write The Word
t o g m	

Write the Word in a Sentence

I will _______ outside.

Don't Forget to Give Yourself the Rates.

Enjoy Learning Sight Words

Color The Word	Trace The Word
has	has

Find and Circle The Word

He has a nice bike.

Has it been a warm spring?

The dog has been good.

she
has
has
hat
has
has
shed
had
has

Read The Word	Write The Word

h   a   r
y   w   s

Write the Word in a Sentence

The boy _______ a ball.

Don't Forget to Give Yourself the Rates.

Enjoy Learning Sight Words

Color The Word	Trace The Word
have	have

Find and Circle The Word

What have you done?

I have had fun.

Do you have a cat?

pet have

have has

have have hats

have he have

Read The Word	Write The Word
h k v e m a g n	

Write the Word in a Sentence

I _______ two dogs.

Don't Forget to Give Yourself the Rates. 

Enjoy Learning Sight Words

Color The Word	Trace The Word
he	he

Find and Circle The Word

He makes me smile.	she he
She likes it, but he does not.	he be she
He and I dance.	the he he her

Read The Word	Write The Word
c e h t	

Write the Word in a Sentence

Jack said ________ will go.

Don't Forget to Give Yourself the Rates. 

Enjoy Learning Sight Words

Color The Word	Trace The Word
her	her

Find and Circle The Word

Her teacher is very tall.

Where is her hat?

Jess went to her house.

her   hat   her   here   hat   her   ear   her   bear

Read The Word	Write The Word
h s r p e t	

Write the Word in a Sentence

My mom likes _______ book.

Don't Forget to Give Yourself the Rates. 

Enjoy Learning Sight Words

Color The Word	Trace The Word
here	here

Find and Circle The Word

Here is my house.

You are there, but I am here.

Here is my dog.

here   here
have   has
here   hats
here   he   here

Read The Word	Write The Word
h e k e m s r g	

Write the Word in a Sentence

I want to stay __________ .

Don't Forget to Give Yourself the Rates. 

Enjoy Learning Sight Words

Color The Word	Trace The Word
his	his

Find and Circle The Word

This is his fish.	his fish
The boy lost his shoes.	is this hat has
His name is Jack.	his house his

Read The Word	Write The Word
a r s h i b	

Write the Word in a Sentence

Sam rides _______ bike.

Don't Forget to Give Yourself the Rates.

Enjoy Learning Sight Words

Color The Word	Trace The Word
I	I

Find and Circle The Word

I have a pet. You and I go to school. Can I have some milk?	a I u a in I I'm I I

Read The Word	Write The Word
I say that I am new.	

Write the Word in a Sentence

Am _____ your friend?

Don't Forget to Give Yourself the Rates. 

Enjoy Learning Sight Words

Color The Word	Trace The Word

Find and Circle The Word

He is in the house.

Did the dog go in the yard?

I put milk in my tea.

into
in
bin
no
inn
on
in
is
in

Read The Word	Write The Word

r n
i t

Write the Word in a Sentence

Can I go _____ the car?

Enjoy Learning Sight Words

Color The Word	Trace The Word
is	is

Find and Circle The Word

She is the teacher.	sir is
Is your dad home?	is is his
It is a funny cat.	mist is bus is

Read The Word	Write The Word
i a g s	

Write the Word in a Sentence

Jane _______ my friend.

Don't Forget to Give Yourself the Rates. 

Enjoy Learning Sight Words

Color The Word	Trace The Word
it	it

Find and Circle The Word

It is a nice day.

Could it be a mouse?

She likes it sweet.

it	if
hit	it
tie	
it	to
of	it

Read The Word	Write The Word
h t i p	

Write the Word in a Sentence

I put _______ in the fridge.

Don't Forget to Give Yourself the Rates. 

Enjoy Learning Sight Words

Color The Word	Trace The Word
like	like

Find and Circle The Word

I would like to go to the zoo.
That dog looks like mine.
We like our friends.

like · like
that · little
love
like · kite
his · like

Read The Word	Write The Word

l h v e
t i k n

Write the Word in a Sentence

We _________ to play.

Don't Forget to Give Yourself the Rates. 

Enjoy Learning Sight Words

Color The Word

look

Trace The Word

look

Find and Circle The Word

I look like my dad.

Look, it's raining.

He will take a look at it.

cool   look   look   little   love   look   like   look   kite

Read The Word

z   o   s   d

l   r   o   k

Write The Word

Write the Word in a Sentence

I like to ________ at books.

Don't Forget to Give Yourself the Rates.

Enjoy Learning Sight Words

Color The Word	Trace The Word
me	me

Find and Circle The Word

Dad picks me up from school.
She likes me.
My friend walks with me.

we   me   me   meat   me   be   gem   me   men

Read The Word	Write The Word
s e m k	

Write the Word in a Sentence

Will you play with _______ ?

Don't Forget to Give Yourself the Rates. 

Enjoy Learning Sight Words

Color The Word	Trace The Word

my

Find and Circle The Word

I put on my shoes.

My friends are very kind.

We will go to my house.

by　　my　　my　　yam　　gym　　me　　my　　mill

Read The Word	Write The Word

m　t　s　y

Write the Word in a Sentence

I can write _______ name.

Don't Forget to Give Yourself the Rates. 

Enjoy Learning Sight Words

Color The Word	Trace The Word
of	of

Find and Circle The Word

Can I have a slice of bread?

He puts one of his socks on.

I am proud of my mom.

of   if   off   of   tie   for   of   from   of

Read The Word	Write The Word
o t s f	

Write the Word in a Sentence

It's a piece _______ cake.

Don't Forget to Give Yourself the Rates. 

Enjoy Learning Sight Words

Color The Word	Trace The Word
on	on

Find and Circle The Word

She puts her coat on.

Can you turn on the tv?

My birthday is on the 12th.

on
or
son
on
not
mom
on
on
no

Read The Word	Write The Word
s n o b	

Write the Word in a Sentence

You can go _______ a boat.

Don't Forget to Give Yourself the Rates. 

Enjoy Learning Sight Words

Color The Word	Trace The Word
Or	or

Find and Circle The Word

| I walk or bike to school.
Do you like it or not?
Mom or dad cooks food. | ear   or
or   on
or
roar   or
or   of |

Read The Word	Write The Word
o k g r	

Write the Word in a Sentence

Is it a dog _______ a cat?

Don't Forget to Give Yourself the Rates. 

Enjoy Learning Sight Words

Color The Word	Trace The Word
said	said

Find and Circle The Word

I said that to her.

He said he knows my name.

'I love cats', said Joe.

said
day
say
said
aid
sad
said
dad
said

Read The Word	Write The Word

s a h d

t z i n

Write the Word in a Sentence

She __________ she likes me.

Don't Forget to Give Yourself the Rates.

Enjoy Learning Sight Words

Color The Word	**Trace The Word**
see	see

Find and Circle The Word

| Can you see me?
I am very smart, you see.
We can see the sun. | she   test
see   see
seek
rest   see
see   bee |

Read The Word	**Write The Word**
g e l s i e	

Write the Word in a Sentence

I _______ the moon.

Don't Forget to Give Yourself the Rates. 

Enjoy Learning Sight Words

Color The Word	Trace The Word
she	she

Find and Circle The Word

Can she ride her bike?

She and I are great friends.

I think she will go to school.

she   the   shed   she   ship   he   she   sheep   she

Read The Word	Write The Word
s h k r w e	

Write the Word in a Sentence

______ is my sister.

Don't Forget to Give Yourself the Rates. 

Enjoy Learning Sight Words

Color The Word	Trace The Word
small	small

Find and Circle The Word

| This is a very small room.
I live in a small town.
Small is the opposite of big. | sam   smile
small   small
mad
say   mall
small   small |

Read The Word	Write The Word
s h k l n k m a p l	

Write the Word in a Sentence

It's a _________ world.

Don't Forget to Give Yourself the Rates.

Enjoy Learning Sight Words

Color The Word	Trace The Word

that

Find and Circle The Word

Where is that ball?

That is my mom.

Did you know that?

this   that   that   the   that   that   what   that   hat

Read The Word	Write The Word

p   h   a   t   t   z   i   s

Write the Word in a Sentence

I know __________ fish swim.

Don't Forget to Give Yourself the Rates. 

Enjoy Learning Sight Words

Color The Word	Trace The Word
the	the

Find and Circle The Word

I see the dog outside.

The cake smells good.

Where is the bus going?

the she
beth the
heat
he they the the

Read The Word	Write The Word
t s e r h i	

Write the Word in a Sentence

I play with ________ toys.

Don't Forget to Give Yourself the Rates. 

Enjoy Learning Sight Words

Color The Word	Trace The Word
they	they

Find and Circle The Word

They will go the park.

I like cats but they do not.

Do they know your dog?

they day say they aid they they dad said

Read The Word	Write The Word
t h k y v z e n	

Write the Word in a Sentence

When do _______ bark?

Don't Forget to Give Yourself the Rates. 

Enjoy Learning Sight Words

Color The Word	Trace The Word
this	this

Find and Circle The Word

This is my name.

You can have this cup.

What is this paper?

this
that
this
this
the
this
his
this
sit

Read The Word	Write The Word
z h v s t a i n	

Write the Word in a Sentence

Do you like __________ hat?

Enjoy Learning Sight Words

Color The Word	Trace The Word
to	to

Find and Circle The Word

She walks to school.

Can I go to Grandma's house?

We are going to the beach.

to   toy

her   to

boat   to   elf

to   of   to

Read The Word	Write The Word
t f v o	

Write the Word in a Sentence

Let's go _______ bed.

Don't Forget to Give Yourself the Rates. 

Enjoy Learning Sight Words

Color The Word

up

Trace The Word

up

Find and Circle The Word

I get up from my bed.

Stand up for your friends.

The kite went up in the sky.

up

pup

cup

up

bud

up

up

pan

upside

Read The Word

u

i

h

p

Write The Word

Write the Word in a Sentence

Look _____ and see the sun.

Don't Forget to Give Yourself the Rates.

Enjoy Learning Sight Words

Color The Word	Trace The Word
very	very

Find and Circle The Word

Thank you very much.

I am very strong.

Her bike is very far from here.

very   your
very   fairy   very
yam   very   ferry   very

Read The Word	Write The Word
v f r y s e d k	

Write the Word in a Sentence

I like you _______ much.

Don't Forget to Give Yourself the Rates. 

Enjoy Learning Sight Words

Color The Word	Trace The Word

we

Find and Circle The Word

We can go cook now.

What will we eat?

We are on the same team.

me   we   we   when   we   elk   he   we   water

Read The Word	Write The Word

q   e

w   k

Write the Word in a Sentence

Where will ______ go?

Don't Forget to Give Yourself the Rates.

Enjoy Learning Sight Words

Color The Word	Trace The Word
what	what

Find and Circle The Word

He gets what he wants.

What will you tell her?

What time is it?

what
what
hat
what
what
what
what
what
who
where

Read The Word	Write The Word
w h k t s y a p	

Write the Word in a Sentence

__________ can I do?

Don't Forget to Give Yourself the Rates.

Enjoy Learning Sight Words

Color The Word	Trace The Word

when

Find and Circle The Word

I see flowers when it's spring.

When did you get here?

We will go when it is time.

what

when

when   we

when

how

when   where   me

Read The Word	Write The Word

s   h   k   n

w   y   e   p

Write the Word in a Sentence

I sleep ____________ I'm tired.

Don't Forget to Give Yourself the Rates.

Enjoy Learning Sight Words

Color The Word	Trace The Word
who	who

Find and Circle The Word

After all, who knows?

Who will go to school?

Tell me who he is.

how who
who what
who
we
wow who who

Read The Word	Write The Word
w h e s y o	

Write the Word in a Sentence

______ lives on a farm?

Don't Forget to Give Yourself the Rates.

Enjoy Learning Sight Words

Color The Word

with

Trace The Word

with

Find and Circle The Word

I go to school with her.

Sit with me.

He likes bread with butter.

with
this
with
with
with
when
we
white

Read The Word

s k t h
w i e p

Write The Word

Write the Word in a Sentence

Will you dance _________ me?

Don't Forget to Give Yourself the Rates.

Enjoy Learning Sight Words

Color The Word

you

Trace The Word

you

Find and Circle The Word

You wear a red jacket.

Can you go with me?

It's for you and me.

you
ours
you
you
sour
your
yam
you
you

Read The Word

t · o · k
y · z · u

Write The Word

Write the Word in a Sentence

Will _______ marry me?

Don't Forget to Give Yourself the Rates.

Enjoy Learning Sight Words

Color The Word

your

Trace The Word

your

Find and Circle The Word

Is that your house?

Your dog is bigger than mine.

You can write your name.

your   ours

your   your

sour

yam   your   you

Read The Word

t o k y

y z u r

Write The Word

Write the Word in a Sentence

This is _______ pet.

Don't Forget to Give Yourself the Rates.

www.ingramcontent.com/pod-product-compliance
Lightning Source LLC
Chambersburg PA
CBHW082041150726
47996CB00016B/3208